NEWS OF THE DAY

NEWS OF THE DAY

POEMS OF THE TIMES

JOHN

Poetic Matrix Press

Poetic Matrix Press
PO Box 1223
Madera, CA 93639
www.poeticmatrix.com
poeticmatrix@yahoo.com

Acknowledgments

I call this collection *News of the Day* to indicate two things. First, some of these pieces were written for specific events; momentary poetic statements of the events of the day. *The Social,* written as a comment on the legacy of the left in the early days of Clinton's Presidency, was one of these pieces, as was *28 Years* written after an invitation by Terry Hertzler to read at a Veteran's Day poetry reading. Second, some pieces were written with specific events in mind like *Voice,* written as a statement about Reagan's dirty war in Nicaragua. Certainly the piece written on hearing of the passing of Allen Ginsberg, that is the dedication piece, is one of these. And *Impeachment,* written about, what else, the Clinton Impeachment, took a long time to write and had to be concise given the excess of the thing itself.

At the 50th Anniversary Beat Conference at NYU in 1994, Gregory Corso lead off his part of the Town Hall Concert with the statement that poets should bring the *news of the day* to the community; with that he read a piece he had written only hours before the concert with his poet's comments on the day's goings on. Since then I've taken it upon myself, prior to a reading or concert, to find that poem that is the *news of the day*, reading it to start off the event. Many of the poems in this collection are of this sort. Other pieces are *news of the day* because the poetry of our time has been a force for articulating the events of our times. Later the events may date the poem but if the event and the poem are worthy then something of lasting value may come along with the piece.

During the development of this manuscript events have unfolded, poems have been written and time has been spent toward a finish that never comes and alas, never will. All of this is never ending, the time, the events and yes the poems.

The poems of the second section, *Poems out of Philosophy,* were written in the aftermath of September 11th and during a period of travel, mostly in the south. They seem to be more philosophical

which, like poems associated with timely events can lend a weight that if not handled well can crush the poetry. This is a chance I am willing to take to say what I feel need be said.

The third section, *Biopoetica*, is really of a different character, leaving the news of the day and philosophical pieces to search a more elusive place. The three sections make something of a whole with jazz as the sound behind them all.

Suggested sound track: <u>Coltrane The Very Best of John</u>, Rhino, 2000. Includes: *Giant Steps, Cousin Mary, Naima, Like Sonny, My Shining Hour, My Favorite Things, Central Park West, Summertime, Mr. Syms, Equinox, Body and Soul.*

Vietnam Early, River, Coming Into Being, Cool Mountain, Some Things Stick, Gathering, Managua, and *Nicaragua 1990* were part of a work with Tomás Gayton titled, <u>Two Races One Face Two Faces One Race</u>, itself a *news of the day* with a black man and a white man intertwining their lives and poetry in the late days of *america*.

An early prose version of *Beat* appeared in <u>Vision Magazine</u>; an early version of *Coming Into Being* appeared in <u>True Wheel</u>; *Blue Night Blues* appeared in <u>The San Diego Writer's Center Anthology, 1996</u>. A number of other pieces have appeared on www.poeticmatrix.com in the *periodic letteR*.

Thanks to James Downs for his careful reading and offer of critique, encouragement and proofing.

John - 2007

to my friends and fellow poets
Terry Hertzler, Tomás Gayton,
and Brandon Cesmat

Contents

PROLOGUE

When This Generation
  -hoffmanoakridge

precisely when this generation
     blindingflash

the moment a single jarring
sets the soul in motion
                    hoffmanoakridge

that common soul that through this
generation moves the apocryphal
moment   synapselightbody

that is the death cold
      shadowbodiesonstonewalls

black as priests robes or god's
immaculate other   expanding
and yes the most inner decision
to survive   yea the only impulse
in it's yet to be foraged history
when it could survive at all
and make a point of light   the
etching of an entire moment
            insideoutside

some precede this moment
          some trail it

some warble on its infinity

DEDICATION

On the Passing of Allen Ginsberg, Poet, Bodhisattva, Reincarnation of William Blake and Walt Whitman, April 6, 1997

Great connector of the poetic voice, life giver, recording, living,
and sharing, in darkness and light, one who travels. Water cast
across space, we travel Buddha field upon Buddha field. Your mother

languishing in a strange world, my mother combing long dark hair
in a world of uncommon shapes and signs, steely foreign life, a world
inhabited during war and fear. I am a casualty of the war of my time,

you and I travel on Buddha path of peace searching for love in the time
of destruction, the time of death taken over by violence and false
grandfathers. A lifeline sits across many worlds, we walk a not deciphered

path yet a common thread of love, soul connection of human, animal,
rock, tree, Buddha's feet, god who could feel, breath of human and the
other, leads us on. Jazz of life, Whitman and Blake, song/voice of

recollection crossing space, human and the other inhabitants of this earth.
You the incarnated voice, me the voice that could not speak, feeling the
groan of the unloved in the middle night. Water of this world, sound of

many voices, you the strong storyteller, me of murmur and silence
occasionally speaking to some stranger you may have missed. You
the lion who took on the world, me a light that shone darkly. But we the

Buddha's noise in the time of uncollected sighs, travelers on a path taken
many times, we say it because it is what is said by us. We speak our
voice or it is choked like the rattle of the dead who did not speak. Tonight

my voice is caught in my chest, the water will not come to carry it out
into the night here on the mountain where truth surrounds me like granite
falling off high valley walls. Communist redemption in the days

of Hale (Be) Bop Comet in the night sky, floating to the dark night, balance of day and dark. The redemption of words in voice and sound, rhythmical scraps of paper floating in a watery quivering chest. Sailing

out across a youthful time and on into the old and the graying morning. Your hair of the beast long and full of lightning, coat of color wrapped skin, luminous soft pools of brown eyes glimmering. Buddha destruction,

flowing long line of reincarnated poets and lovers, peace walkers on the road traveled by love, incarnated into the body of god's multitude of daughters and sons, crossed and crisscrossing the land absconded by

Moloch who drowns the meek and the strong at the same time. We are caught in the web of the same old misapprehension of good and ill, forgetful that this is the life of our world and we are the million fingers

of god, the finger nails of the Buddha. Words are floating evidence of our body, circulating essence of soul in communion with the mind that is empty, they fall to earth and grow into the shadow of our longing, we

inhabit them with our sisters of the other, our dead brothers sailing out. We are the concrete mass body waiting to flee into the discorporal night, the discorporal spirit waiting to stretch into the body of desire. We bless

our creation and evaporate into the empty mind of the universal void, into the grace of god, the Tao, the Buddha field, into the comet's light leaving the April night sky. Now and then Allen, we find you hidden

in the lines of your poems, speaking out to us, urging us to do what poets and artists must do. And, as you said, even if all of this comes to nothing in 100 or 200 years, make this a better place for all we meet,

on this love path of uncommon shapes and signs, traveling through this strange world.

News of the Day

I

They haven't put up barricades, yet,
the streets still alive with faces,
lovely men & women still walking there,
still lovely creatures everywhere,
in the eyes of all the secrets of all
still buried there,
Whitman's wild children still sleeping there,
Awake and walk in the open air.

Lawrence Ferlinghetti
from *Populist Manifesto*: <u>Endless life: Selected Poems</u>

To Miles Davis

Inside of different lights, a new
born reverie, black capped and wing'ed
crossing like memory on teal-darkened
rooftops   touching somber   vague
ladies the color of sorcerer dreams.

Walking in the cool, steel, vacuous night,
buried in a feelingless hum, pressed inside
a castled space with long, low, lean towers.
Bowling alley sounds at two a.m.,
Greyhound Bus to the Blackhawk bitter end.

Climbing into brass horns and intimately
sheathed embraces. Smoothness Miles,
smoothness, gliding in on ribs and lungs
and long sighs, speaking with inner friends
animating worlds unseen.

Dragons rear   inside of orange lights
before the sacrificial revolution.
Death is walled inside of schools
and homes between the Shoreview workers
ghetto and the Cadillacs of Hillsborough.

Who ever heard of tacos or knew
a Tarasco face and we live as
white folks live and black man never
would be black and we would dance
as tears and rage bound his ribs to ours.

Bodies of rare substance, crashing
images of suburban war burning fears
leaping Zen poem sung by the war dead

bathing nerves somewhere in North Beach.
Sprayed with sooty jazz in the Blackhawk
sewer where the drapes hung like rags
and the music stung like love   and
Miles Davis blew warm hellish feelings,

cageless as the fog on the damp, damp
                              coastal hills.

Gregory Corso
Jazzaz Beat Concert 1994

Oh, if only I had the hipster
voice with a sense of humor
like Ginsberg, the bald old queer
hip, beat poet, stand up comic trickster.

If I could just turn
my tragic, dramatic, war weary,
serious, sexual, revolutionary,

hippie, long hair, radical,
want to save the world, life
into something that David Letterman
and Jay Leno
could steal monologues from.

Arsenio can't do it, he's back
out here with me doing one nighters.

Dennis Miller's goin' the other way
from doing tongue in cheek Miller beer
commercials to doing my old stand-up
social commentary.

Watch it Dennis, keep it light
the folks don't like it straight
at the solar plexus.

Keep it light, hit the funny bone.

Like Corso said
keep it short
keep it funny
and get off the stage.

Beat

Beat Conference - 1994

When traveling it seems we've got to get high first,
loosen up, let go, doesn't matter how.
This time flyin' on a 747 at 30,000 feet
talkin' to Cindy from Philly.

Sees my book on Timothy Leary,
asks if I got into him, LSD and all.
I say, "everyone finds a way to get high,
a way to find the place of spirit.
Here you are, a flight attendant on this big spaceship,
helping people get high over and over."

Flew into New York City, haven't been here in 20 years—
takin' the "A" train from JFK to the Chelsea Hotel—
thinkin' of Ellington, and Poitier and Newman, in *Paris Blue*.

Spent a couple of nights at the Chelsea,
where Dylan Thomas died, Sid killed Nancy,
and Arthur C. Clark wrote *2001* — death and life.

Went to New York for *The Beat Generation Conference*,
billed as the 50th Anniversary of a literary movement
that changed *american* life—for good or ill.

After doing Tai Chi in the Park at Washington Square,
a native comes up to me, says, "sink down."
Tai Chi teachers always say, "sink down."
Sink down he told me, you've got to get the legs into it,
so the trunk is strong and sturdy, so the flowering
can occur again with new seeds scattered on the breeze,
        "blowin' in the wind".

In New York, Allen Ginsberg, Gregory Corso, Michael McClure,
Ted Joans, Anne Waldman, Joyce Johnson, Jan Kerouac,
Ray Manzarek, Hunter S. Thompson, David Amram, Joanne Kyger,

Cecil Taylor, Ed Sanders, many more, connecting the jazz blowin',
dope smokin', street singin', new thinkin', sex freein', poet breathin',
Zen sittin', new life, *on the road* with *doctor sax* and the
dharma bums, a strange *howl* across the gray flannel *u s of a*.

Lookin' for that singular jazzline that will blow all
the old uptight, school goin', anti-commie, post nuclear,
soul killin' nonsense out there where it'll get transformed
into the pure love soul sweet sax line John Coltrane playin'
        My Favorite Things.

Tomás and I takin' in the jazz scene,
checkin' out Clark Gayton
playin' with the Charlie Mingus Big Band.

Diggin' the New York street poet
at a funky Jazz Club with flirtatious blond and brunette.

Young woman standing on the bar at closing
singing *New York New York* with Sinatra on the jukebox.

Greenwich Village, Cafe Reggio, the Lion's Head,
Stonewall Park, The Blue Note.

Below the Arch in Washington Square the Park is jamming'.
Beat ladies in black, hippylonghairpeacesign,
Hare Krishna chalk artist, Tai Chi Taoist healer,

Madison Avenue yuppie strippin' down to T-shirt and blue jeans,
slacker and rapper, hangin' out together.

The 50s, 60s, 70s, 80s, all here in the 90s,
        passin' the joint back and forth.

Music, art, poetry, healing, the world beat, the world soul,
traveling on a thin violet line, heading for the next millennium.

Carin and the Beat Chicks
Beat Conference - 1994

Listening to "Beat Chicks",
Hattie, Joyce, Carolyn, Jan,
I thought of you.

I don't know where you are now
but you did the road way back.

You didn't hit the road with the guys
you did it yourself, catchin' rides from
California to Iowa—

I remember a photograph of you
sittin' on the porch of an old Iowa farm.

What our older sisters couldn't do,
you and your sisters did years later.

Your road is still way out there.

Some day you'll tell your younger
sisters how it was in the 70s,
hitch hikin' on the road
in the *u s of a* without fear.

No fear that your brothers on the road
would harm you.

Tell your sisters
that it was this way once,

When the innocent
were free
and we did   love   each other.

For My Brother Craig

Thirty years ago brother
we pulled into New York City
gas tank on empty
wallet on empty
eating saltines.

Spreading out along the highway
from San Francisco to Pensacola,
Asheville, across the Blue Ridge Parkway,
the spine of Shenandoah.

Traveling with Steinbeck and Charlie,
the jazzline from Bird to Kerouac.

What did we know then,
what do we know now
30 years and a lot of blacktop later.

Washington Square with Dylan and Baez,
hundreds of youth of our time
looking for a fix
that would open up
Satori
carried in my backpack
inside the *Way of Zen*.

Who could tell,
maybe I couldn't get it with my mind
'cause my belly was too deep into it.

Today with some of the Beat masters
listening to how it was—no that's wrong—
it's only the way it was if it's the way it is,
that's the whole point isn't it,

it's just the way it is.
On the dais
talking about Beat history
who met who, when, where,

Allen and I got caught
eye to eye.

We stayed for a moment
had a meeting.

We've been together
all these years
he and I
and a thousand others
a million others
seeing what is out there
takin' it in
saying it one way or another.

It's a whole in the heart
from a long way back,
way back before today
before
you and I ran across this country
not knowing a thing.

Who knows where it comes from
where it started
or where it will end.

Of course it won't end,
even when all of this is seen for what it is
a dream
a place to rest
a place to say hello to our sisters and brothers
on the long, long road
that is not.

Just our life, our living
swirling
twisting
flyin' through
this glory space we live in.

30 years brother
and I love you like all the roads,
mountains,
the cities
we fled through,
wandering,
just knowing this was where we had to go.

Its like a heart beat
how you gonna get away from it anyway.

Sittin' in a coffee house
on 6th Avenue in the Village
and tears come to me
like soft rain outside the window.

All the young
and the old

streaming by.

II

for every revolutionary must at last will his own destruction
rooted as he is in the past he set out to destroy

Diane Di Prima
from *Revolutionary Letters 12*: <u>Pieces of a Song</u>

Vietnam - early

Soon after settling in Long Binh, Pat and I
head into Bien Hoa. Pat, a tall good-natured man
from Hollywood, wanted to be an LA cop. He's smart
beneath layers of asphalt, stop lights and movie stars.

We move off the GI track, down alleys, on the people's
streets, olive drab fatigues stand out.

We walk with stories from home. Young boy moves toward
us. In a joking voice, we wonder if he carries a live grenade
and will blow our three bodies into a union
of blood and bone as we have heard.

We pass beyond, his brown eyes give no clue.

Another street and the church stands out, Pat is Catholic
and must go in, I follow.

Small nuns in black and white—no English—from the north—
fled with many orphans—settled here—little money—fifty or
so children—many infants—cribs line the large hall—cribs
with no mattress—always hot—many flies through open windows.

We talk as best we can, older children come up to us and
soon we are bodies with many feet and hands.

Inside white stucco walls—an arch leads somewhere, outside
the ground is bare, a few trees—I don't know the names—like
the children—brown eyes and brown hair—white dress or
cotton shirt, bare feet on dirty ground.

Pat returns many times, I come and sit with pen and paper
and sketch caricatures of the little ones—some shy
and will only approach after the drawing is done—others pose

and demand to see—all are noisy and share in the overlap
of what we are and where our worlds have carried us, each with
a spark from which I draw, a stance of a movement, the tilt of a head
or the shape of an eye, a pulling back or the smell that reveals.

Someone sees, somewhere the drawing.

Each time the gate is opened and I am a tree and their roots
are my ground.

Today, our eyes stare   into a common sky.

River

The word river sounds like the river

But

not only does it sound like the whole
river that runs through Vietnam
through rice paddies and jungle
and villages because that's what language
is supposed to do

But it

sounds like the whole
river that runs through

Bangkok Temple

Flying out of Saigon like a man on death row lied to about a reprieve.
Bangkok smelled like sweat off a long line of children playing hard.

The first night, cabarets and restaurants, dark night streets, light
from inside sucking out the daily rain of tracers and armed forgetting.

Before sleep, rolling with round Buddha hills, caught in gold
broken memory, her eyes closely held.

She told a long convoluted story about family, life and friends
in a far off village, bringing a mirror into focus in this city of users.

Her name was Ally, her long all night story keeping another carrier
of the war dead away from her jade temple.

Climbing 400 steps to the top, temples ascend everywhere
in the daytime, gone in the night where she can't be found.

Looking out over the city there are clouds even where the sun
shines, I have 400 more steps to climb at least.

How foolish these soldiers look decked out in the tour boat,
cameras ready, clean white shirt startling like the day.

But the floating market dances on the head of a pin,
flowers strewn on the water, the river flowing.

Smell of cooking food in dugout canoes on the waterway,
in the air, keeping war from these waters.

In front of the mirror her reflection looks back, she stands looking
side to side admiring her body, her breasts, her face looking out.

Flying back across green jungle, the plane quiet with engines throbbing, roiling up from the jungle a familiar smell that blocks reflection.

A joke that keeps the condemned laughing rises into the air, plane touches the ground at Ton Son Nuyt, eyes glancing back and forth.

Coming Into Being

I'm having trouble finding an emotional opening into memory
and into the world that is in formation, the coming into being.

Much is out there now, many secret lives laid open, the past
and present, the future dreamed, all of this is out there now.

One day I'm a stone quarrier, back broken on the pyramids of the sun,
the next a soldier with Rommel, my life severed just before defeat.

This time a hod carrier for a Salvadorian concrete master watching
his tears flow; now a soldier in the 407th Transportation Group
                        just before Tet, the truck burning.

Here I dance to catgut strings at a Mexican wedding with a black
haired girl.

The next day I'm a security guard on the USS Enterprise,
my death comes early in the episode. Now I am a post-nuclear
vegetable seller with patches of skin peeling.

I marry now a peasant girl on the edge of Sherwood Forest,
before Robin Hood, or a young girl with long red hair in an
Irish town when the snakes were there.

This time, working in the fields, picking grapes in 110 degree heat
before Montezuma failed the people. Now on board a Galaxy Class
Cruiser doing the work that Captains and Officers won't do.

Or standing at the rail of a troop transport, 20 days at sea watching
fresh strawberries and ice cream being dumped overboard from the
Officer's Mess, while eating powdered eggs and nonfat dry milk
solids one day from Cameron Bay and the death of a million
brothers and sisters.

I asked the Sergeant about those strawberries and ice cream, he said there wasn't enough left over from the 200 officers for the 5000 men
stacked six deep in the holds.

We congregate in a big hanger deep in the ship in 120 degree heat watching an old Bob Hope movie, the one where Step 'n Fetchit shuffles across the screen, where 300 men sit on the hot steel floor, half of them Black and the room gets tenser than a teenager on a first date.

And no one speaks.

Today I walk with 250,000 children, women and men, down the streets of San Francisco, from the past and the future screaming   crazy.

Le Ly Hayslip

You spoke of bare feet on the ground of your village,
                    feet touching earth.

Seventeen years and you wore no shoes,
                            feet touching earth.

How that connection gave you your world,
earth coming though the soles of your feet.

Hips deep.

Mud of rice fields,
mud of your life.

Your ancestors walked with you,
feet touching earth.

You said how
   shoes and pavement stop the connection
        roots cannot penetrate,
                        we skim the top unbalanced,
      no anchors, no place

                    down.
Energy builds in the belly like steel helmets of war.

For a time I wore no shoes, my feet spread on asphalt,
                        hot
            in 105 degree Valley heat,
      breaking up concrete, coils moving like mud
            through sidewalk cracks,
                    head coming off.

I ran like a deer one time near the grottos on the Fresno river,
grass green with sweat, feet cut bloody   marking granite.

Each foot   finding the right place   on a narrow deer path
   above the
                              diving pool.

For a time I knew how your feet   moved   over village ground.

I knew when the earth comes up   a dark   dark rose   how my

body

follows contour of hills   bending as feet   touch the earth

          running.

Cool Mountain

I came up on them in the cool mountain night
huddled beneath the eves of the rain soaked cabin

Sunshine and Hippie squatting in the blue shadow
sobs coming from the dark figure between them

I start to go up
I knew it before
I remember the green fatigues
combat boots bloused at the ankles
hair not yet grown out

Only three years from the fall of Saigon
Rob was one of the last to leave—
its been jumbled for a long time—
still wearing jungle fatigues years later

I start to approach but Sunshine motions me away
hair down his back   golden and bright
Hippie leaning over   long hair tied behind
three of them making a tight circle
keeping the tears between them

They lift him up out of dampness
hot wet arms and legs laid out
over knee deep rice fields

Years earlier watching a senseless war movie
tears flood me like the afternoon monsoon
I call Rich and sit in the basement
drink a six-pack   he holds our circle
'til the steel bands loosen

Now they hold Rob tightly
in the cool dark mountain shadows
lifting him up so he won't fall
into darkness   broken

III

Both are late because empty thereof,
Empty is light, empty is dark,
  what's difference between emptiness
  of brightness and dark?

Jack Kerouac
from *105th Chorus*: <u>Mexico City Blues (242 Choruses)</u>

Planet

At 10,000 feet from
San Diego to LA.

Ocean below, pebbly
clouds, sun at my rear.

Boats and buildings, you know,
like Monopoly pieces.

Another airplane
off to the east.

Earth so big,
no wonder the plane flies.

It could just fly off
into space.

Like a bullet gone
astray.

Ben Webster

Letting go of shady images, smoky
bars and rain soaked streets,
Mike Hammer lost in the night.

Tall downtown buildings—
street light shadow image,
smoky place on ribs and long sighs—
piano string before the felt hammer hits.

I remember a night long ago,
sitting in the dark looking out the bay window,
sound of a moving baseline—
neighborhood reachin' in.

Old gray man—
piano riff rising easy off of blue pavement.

I'd never seen this middle class suburb
like it had a rhythm
'til I got inside the breath sound
soft and cool,
Ben Webster sax
beatin' out a dark place,
no matter where it sits—

Behind us
all.

Night and Day & Night

Each day
a big overbearing Mantra
keeps me moving along
at its own pace.

First
the kids
like sweet Cherubic alarms.

Bright nighttime faces
open to the day.

Time to roll over from sleep and dreaming
to see the night's effect
on youthful bodies.

Reach for my bathrobe,
trundle down circular stairs.

Smell of Nicaraguan coffee
stirring warm odors
in the morning air.

The day-to-day comes like an unsought place,
rocks on fire,
a turn of childish laughter
seeping back into the unavailable night.

After the long days running
the night is still,
a gray curtain hanging straight and cool—
a place of desireless longing
nothing in particular,
Just a longing of the night
to boil us down
to essential places.

Standing as it were on the edge of the day
the edge of this
ready for that.

The long descent.

Careless—

Where desire cannot enter.

Where we are pulled along
by a great Mantra—
of sound

& music.

Soft Night

rain on a roof
metal ringing up and down in front of
concrete played steely in the background, voices

'cross the way sing up slightly and the long rolling sound,
tires on asphalt pools, night rolling
years of cold water, the flash behind a young gray
shadow

people forgetting the way they came
into the world, the gift giving and the blood
spilt, everywhere

Night

The night brings me
Up out of pavement
Into a place of stars
City lights off the sky
Bar door opens
Red lady dancin'
Sharp cold night.

Ensenada - After a Day Drive

A thief amongst potholes
and taco stands, broken wood
and elements of glass.

A smell I cannot get at,
dust everywhere I turn,
on leaves, cars, windows.

Fish tacos and many blankets—
five dollars and the colors
pink, green, and soft blue.

Round large hole, water blowing through,
La Bufadora deep beneath stones—young woman walks
on high heels, in tights, look behind—
who is the thief who takes the alter.

Six children smiling in the rain.

Old man I flee from, old women I can't get to,
la curandera knows but can't make it.

One more pothole and I'll scream.

One more taco.

There, a young Indio girl, clean pants,
overlaid dress, hair absolutely shining;
gave her a coin, she gave me a polished
stone in a Pleistocene river—a bell shaped stone.

Look back, she smiles,
I want to follow her—
she is gone.

Streets still broken, fish tacos, pescado,
more stones, weeds, paint,
ten thousand pot holes.

Some Things Stick

Marquette Frye, whose arrest Ignited the Watts Riot in 1965,
dies at the age of 42.
LA Times, Thursday, Dec. 25, 1986

Some things stick

The moment is clear
events before and after remain unrecognizable

No reason

White boy, artist, middle class suburban
seven days a week in an all white church.

But here, can't remember his name
or how we met, Ventura 1965.
Black man janitor at a
greasy spoon on main street.
Went to meet him one afternoon,
can't remember the day.

Good man, desire like a new coat,
wanted to do something real,
can't remember what.

Twenty years and I haven't thought of him
maybe two or three times
but today, when Marquette Frye died
he comes back clear and pure like
the high-pitched harmonic of a song
driven
burning orange   heat
embellishment through some
voice of the radio man.

Standing in the greasy spoon
maybe five o'clock, waiting to leave.
Black man janitor friend
walks up and the radio man voice from Watts
stops us all in place.

Tells us this fire from the world beneath ours
has taken over white boy, artist, suburban
middle class, seven days a week and it is
the glory of cars burnin'
and windows breakin'
and television sets being carted off and
columns of smoke risin' above the high rise
skyline and no one in the room knows that it
was Marquette Frye who died twenty-one years
later not even knowin' how something underneath
him needed a way to the sky.

I'll bet you now Black man janitor friend is
what he wanted, 'cause he had a desire strong
enough to see fires in the sky and keep goin',
blood in another's eye and keep livin',
and then I didn't even know that I didn't know
what it really was about.

Three years later, workin' at a car wash,
just back from NAM,
heard that Martin Luther King had been shot,
still didn't know, like the mind had been
saved from detailing all the pains of the body,
but I found my eyes full of tears and I didn't
know why Marquette Frye, Black man janitor
friend, and white boy artist were cryin', but
there they were.
Twenty-one years later saw the jewels put back
on the crown through the life of another man
from Watts.

But this time, go on Marquette Frye, open up
        the sky.

48

Long Lines

I've been in these lines before
every few years I get
this connection renewed

Long time back it was the *Army Induction Center*
long line of brothers from the
Midwest   South   LA and beyond

We stood shoulder to shoulder comparing
skin color   the shape of thighs   whether torsos
were long or lean   bulky with muscle or fat

Wondering what lay behind those opaque
eyes   how far back did we have to go before
blue eyes   green eyes   brown eyes melted away

Later the lines were mixed with women and children
the color bronze and chocolate   paler skin the
minority   more how the whole world looked

It was easy   natural   food stamps
and the goods they buy are the same
no matter the mouths they feed

Baseball caps the predominate head
gear of that peculiar look of the working
class white male born in the seventies

Longish hair   scraggly beard   blue jeans
flannel shirt open over a white T-shirt
and that cap   marijuana leaf on the front

Sisters and brothers have come together
to draw supplies   meager though they be
from the social world they have created

Dirty walls and ash tray old and unclean
do not smell of the best our culture
has to give   but they will serve now and then

I may be back again   some day I'll see it
shining around us and shining in that
deep place   behind the many colored eyes

Eloquent Dead

Exhibit of Sulawese Art UCLA Wright Gallery

I look on the Tau Tau
figures of Sulawese
and see in their eyes
confusion and loss.

Young man comes by
and says, "they are stolen,
it is a live culture
and they are stolen."

My heart races with
the dragonfly over the waterways
of Sulawese.

Bopal

TV news report
of the Union Carbide pesticide leak, 1984
that poisoned and killed two thousand
in Bopal India.

This was immediately cut to a bombastic ad
for Vacation Holiday Cruises
to various parts of the world.

This image, one on the other,
close to the new language of the earth,
so close to the earth in speech
that it cannot be misunderstood.

Close to one heart beating in another.

Gathering

We gathered at Quel Fromage* after Christmas as the bombs fell,
tiny children of Panama, their gifts coming.

This time we gathered at Soho reading poetry.

The small children screaming blood in the Baghdad bunker
are part of no conspiracy of history, they cannot indict
either one of their raging killers.

I remember a boy in Estelí playing with a cow
near the old theater while M-16 rounds tear
the heart from his older brothers
and a young girl with ancestral eyes at the orphanage
in Bien Hoa, standing as B-52s turned her village
into shrieking vapor.

We read again, collect clothing for the children on the cold
avenues of Tijuana, greeting the Buddha, homeless
and forgetful on San Diego streets,

Finding charred roots and the curling up,

Finding in the chilled air a conduit to the future, a believable rain
to water these children's   deep places.

*San Diego's oldest coffeehouse

Managua

The city is dark, Orion's
belt is visible,
I must find the
Mayan name* for it.

On the streets the children
play, parents sit
around open doors and
wrought iron gates.

Black and white television
screens blink out and some
are being viewed.

Restaurants and bars
in the neighborhood are active,
food from street vendors is good.
Enchiladas with thick fried
tortillas, beef and white rice
and a pinch of Cole slaw with
hot sauce on two palm leaves.

I am caught by smells and
by life in front of doors.

The roof is communal
and the rooms shared.
The black sky cannot fall
and the bright lights
Cannot go out.

I call to you across the
night sky as we agreed.

*Cosmic Turtle

Nicaragua 1990

Its election morning at 5:30 a.m., I'm
sitting on the street in Estelí waiting
for Jack and the film crew. It's cloudy
and cool with a bit of a breeze. Across the
street a German Shepherd looks at me. A
few people are out this early. The church
bell rang a minute ago, a call to mass.
El gallo is busy.

It is a morning with a sense of calm.
I haven't seen any military activity today although
I saw many patrols yesterday as we drove to
el coopertivo in las montañas.

Voice
-for Brandon

I look to Nicaragua and see the poet
Ernesto Cardenal

Rigoberto Lopez Perez
he is a poet

I am a poet

Dark soil   canopy of dark   dark green

I know now the protection of the word
Why the Nicaraguan's sing
Why the poets speak the word
    wrap the people in a cover
    of words   to hold

            the dead
    who died by Somoza   who

            died
    by the Contra's bullets   again

House with Mayan rooms
room of the Catholic   Indian   African—
women who speak the Caribbean lilt—
Spanish walls   and the gold

House of Sandino   communista
Ché   Fidel   Fonséca—revolucionario
who loves the people and gives blood
in the life of sisters and brothers
I know why the people sing
cover the children in a love song of words

Poetry is not only a literary discipline

It is myriad pulsing
in the night time of lovers

A mother's breath sound
in her child's heart

Rhythm of nerves
dancing in space

The word before there was voice
to transmit the word

Truth talking to truth
glowing bodies in the gold light of morning

Poetry is the earth covering her own
in a green and gold   mantle   of love

IV

The weight of the world
   is love.
Under the burden
   of solitude,
under the burden
   of dissatisfaction

  the weight,
the weight we carry
   is love.

Allen Ginsberg
from *Song*: <u>Collected Poems 1947-1980</u>

Blue Night Blues

Spent all day
drivin' my car
through the blues

Black top drum beat
goin' somewhere

Turnin' corners
headin' for a date
a job
a rendezvous

Stoppin' at the *Wiki-Up*
met a drummer friend

Talked to Ken at *Earth Support*
about love and the land
that quintessential combination

Worker's diggin' up the boulevard
rhythm of jackhammer
and concrete fallin'

Water gushing
cement trucks dropping
slippery green mix
into
mysterious holes

Muscles
ache tonight

Down by the bay
blue water turned orange

by the almost gone sun
Traffic goin' east
or north
or south

Suits headin' home
to that same old news

Can't wait to put on
Miles
or Bird
or Montovani

When jazz is the background of a city
it becomes a jazz place
in the back of your
blues mind

A hole opens—
foot starts beatin' out a rhythm

Muscle aches give way to
Nighttime settlin' nerves

Jazz place—
a ground against the
crazy pace of the city

Droppin' off the world
Swirlin' in the rhythm space
set up by
the blue night blues

Caught between my ribs

And you

28 Years
News of the Day – Veteran's Day 1995

Pat, Rich, and I had only been discharged
out of Fort Lewis Washington a few days
when we decided to go see
John Wayne in the *Green Berets.*

We thought it would be a lark
to see how Hollywood saw NAM.

Grauman's Chinese Theater was packed—
we sat in the front row, necks craned back
John Wayne 20 feet tall.

The opening scene cracks us up—
three short hair, thick necked vets
laughing in the front row
everyone else silent as patriots.

On the tarmac at Tan Son Nyut,
the US Air Force base near Saigon
where Pat, Rich, and I
drove 3, 4 times a week for a year,

Solidified napalm—
leaking out as F-100s are loaded
ready to drop bombs on bodies of tiny girls—
stood 6 frightening inches deep
everywhere.

On screen we watch
a perfectly drilled platoon,
in full gear, march shoulder to shoulder
up and down the air strip.
Charlie's Hollywood snipers ready
for the cue to take off their heads.

Later we went to Santa Monica beach,
Pat and I, a couple of ladies,
and a jug of Sabastiani.

Walked out on the rock jetty,
drank, laughed, and hollered
a year of body bags sunk in the middle
ground in our guts.

Drank so much Pat had to carry me back
to the motel room.

Never did get it out.

Later, during antiwar work
couldn't bring myself to become a member
of *Vietnam Veterans Against the War*.

Worked with activist friends,
organizing, demonstrating,
didn't really want to be a Vietnam Vet.

Eventually I had to admit
I had that new disease—
Post-Traumatic Stress Disorder.

All the symptoms fit—
Couldn't stay with one thing,
divorced, hated steady jobs, woke up in sweats,
couldn't stand in lines.
Went off to the Sierra foothills with a Mexican girl.

In 1984 I finally took on being a Vet
tired of Reagan's dirty war
in Nicaragua.
Went into classrooms
talked about "The Horror",
military stupidity,
the Vietnamese people.

Listen to myself
disconnect until emotions
hook in and I leave
drained to bone,
depleted of charge.

Never knew if my reality
got past their image of Rambo
and Chuck Norris.

During the Gulf War
got invited to read poetry and talk about NAM
at the Performing Arts School.

Images from TV,
the call to patriotism,
rhetoric of support.

Introduced as a Vietnam Vet
the class applauds and cheers,
skin hairs raise, nerves fill.

Felt for a moment what
it might have been like
to be in the service of a good people
who needed the power and sacrifice
of its young women and men
to protect and secure their lives.

Men and women who could come back
to the love and appreciation of that people.

But that was only for a moment,
I left disoriented.

Left them in silence
with a description of a government and a people
gone crazy.

I've done little talking since then.
Still sure of the error of my year in NAM,
and the error of the past 28 years.

Shaved off my mustache the other day—

Grew it early in my
year in-country.
My sergeant, a real asshole,
was disappointed,
good troops in his mind
were clean shaven.

Haven't seen my upper lip
in 28 years.
Can't decide if this face was there before—

Probably not
that face never made it back.

What's there now has to deal
with everything
that's gone on—

In between.

Mekka Java Coffee House

Downtown Mekka Java

Sittin' on the rain wet deck

City jumpin' all around

Helicopter overhead
Shinin' spot lite on 5th Avenue

Cops bustin' brothers on the street

Mekka Java
Low light and coffee steamin' up the night

Jazz on the corner
Love cuttin' through

Talkin' 'bout the day light conversation
Burst of desire
Buddha in rags
Hot moment of passion

Women and men

All shapes

Goin' down

The Social
News of the Day - Jazzaz Beat Concert 1995

I've been caught for weeks
in a hard place
in the center of my chest.

Like 10,000 fingers
that will have their way.

Until something sets me off
water on the move—

A song from *Pocahontas*
sung with my kids—

My wife coming home too late—

Or a maudlin line by Albert Brooks
to Meryl Streep in a forgettable film.

I tighten up—alone
or I release,
I tighten up—with friends
or I release.

My lady told me it's all right
to hang out in this place of chaos,
uncommitted
where energy is loosened.

Bush is gone
the left is without
moral indignation.

Clinton becomes President
the militia rises as the
oppressed of the nation—
Oklahoma City, Waco, Ruby Ridge.

This great social lady,
is giving us a ride.

We'll break, we always do,
she breaks our complacency,
she overwhelms the sureness
of our lives—
she breaks out.

Backtracking on Affirmative Action,
cutting welfare,
hitting old folks hard.

It depends I guess
on where I stand.

South Africa, Nicaragua,
El Salvador, Sendero,
only Cuba gets an occasional
write-up lost as we are in
the white Bronco, Ito's beard, OJ's gloves,
Marcia's dew,
and Nicole's broken, battered face,
Goldman's anonymity shattered by his father's rage.

Was it because OJ is black, rich, had the dream team,
bad prosecution, Fuhrman, a good jury, a bad jury,
innocent,
400 years of oppression,
ran too many yards in Buffalo.
White males sink into racism
hated by everyone.

I sit on the porch, breathe deep,
take pine trees, crickets,
the occasional owl
& the oil of the night
onto ribs;
the heaviness is not oppressive,
it is the blanket of the Dark Madonna.

The pain has come back stronger
and is harder to dispel.

A Mexican family drowns in the Tijuana river—
gringo politicians want to put up 3 fences on the border.

Am I crazy.
Caught in the imbalance,
caught
in the
dis ease
of the social game.

Where do we find
the poetry of our lives?

The play of opposites

On the thin skin

Of you

And I.

Hillcrest

Midmorning strings play across my chest
rhythmic avenue dancing on.

Last night it rained hard—
under patio floodlights I could see many water drops
bounce off my Acacia plant.

This morning clouds are huge but scattered
heavy and boiling gray—open to the sun
and the cool spring mother.

Down 5th Avenue it's like a street sweeper
had gone by—steel slick shots of color—
clean and well cared for.

Young black woman leading her child,
breasts free behind a white tank top
brought me up out of the wet pavement.

In front of the Quel a young man,
dressed in white and black,
with a hand brush and soapy water
scrubs the red sidewalk.

Seems Parisian in the way he's at it—
like seeing Paris through the eyes of Renoir and Degas.

Thelma says hello to me at the Union Bank
drive-up tellers window,
says she hasn't seen me in awhile.

That's true, been goin' to the Laurel Street Branch,
don't say it's inconvenient coming to a drive-up bank
without a car—but that's the reason.

On 4th Avenue this time a tall blond in a green sweater
and white shorts passes by
nods
seems unsure of the daytime propriety of letting
breasts – unencumbered – sway to the rolling sound
of buses moving, car horns sounding and
red lights turning always to green –
but there she is.

Iced Cap and Poppy Seed Cake and a quiet place to sit
and let this morning
slowly turn the day.

Tijuana

9:00 PM
streets are full everywhere
same as the daytime

Turistas in shops
on Revolución

Children and mothers –
sloe eyed Indio girl
selling Chicles on the corner

Cowboy in leather boots and blue jeans
girl friend
draped arm
bare shoulder
comin' to the city for the night life jammin'

Disco roof top bar dancin'
jazz beat
neon light
black shadow skyline
city playin' sex line

Downtown summer night
semiarid coastal
deep ocean water
low   moaning hills

Dinner –
more for gringos than locals

Red wine from Santo Tomás

Colorful talk
from the night side ladies
at red draped tables

In the long
cool

Summer night

For Blue Print at Croces

Tonight the jazz is hot
Croce's hittin' the jazzline

Live like the heat inside my jacket
Armpits alive with light
and fire

Bassline ridin'
the smooth brown neck
on that standing bass

There are colors here
hot blues and reds
filtered between the bassline
and drum beat rhythm
callin' me

Yea
let the bassline
lean in
from a hidden place

Cornet sailin' through
carryin' you to me
on that
wing walkin'
wall of sound

I'm at a place where
there is jazz
nothing else is there
just the sound on nerves
hittin' up against
a soulful place

Pianoman talks to me tonight
pianoman and bassline
walkin' through me
tonight

Talkin' to me

Raisin' the call in me
gettin' into that sound
that turns into colors
cracklin' around

Rhythman took us away
yes he did
and you pianoman
yeah
you got rhythman
and bassline goin' strong—
set up behind that
Coronet sailin' through

You come out
a pyrotechnical flame
burnin' through the keyboard strollin'

Through cracks left by
drumstick on skins
cat gut cuttin' into finger tips

Set up that run of light color
coaxed off nerves—blues and reds,
orange and green as grass—
turning' my insides into a
holy other place

Cornet sailin' through
you got the blue print on me

Yes you do

Impeachment

Waiting in the late days of the twentieth century
the trial going on and on

Something sits just outside
my understanding

Wants us all back where the law
is the domain of the god who cannot feel

The world of the *soul killin' nonsense*
of the mid 1950s

Who would go back
to that time and place
if they had a choice

Black man janitor friend?—Vietnamese orphan?—
men in long lines?—Rigoberto Lopez Perez?—
young Black women leading her child?

Night on San Diego Bay

Magenta sky
from lights turned to air

In the last days the sky
will turn
the color of love

Water – ribbon of the city –
curling from the skyline
dark like the under sides of ships

Generator colors
power river and high dams
real life work
from the workman's hands

Glass buildings
climbing from cyberspace
sides steely
glass sun hot
hard orange
color
the purple of dusk

Steely lights
turn
steely gray

And we are magenta
air
magenta air   of love

POSTLOGUE

Falling off El Capitan and the World Trade Center

I can only say this as it came to me
first in Yosemite after hearing about
a climber on El Capitan

When rappelling down the face he had
failed to tie a knot in the end of the rope
and rappelled off the end

A clear preternaturally clear moment
that a great mistake had occurred and then he fell
3000 feet to the soft valley floor

Petals of violet stacked points of light
wings glisssando in the barely utterable day
grassy hands pushing off the foaming granite

And again as pictures of the Trade Center Tower
is shown and those sweet souls clinging to the side
of the building as flames ate up the interior

The lucitity of the moment
that a great wrong had occurred
and they fell

But the earth gave way
the valley floor   the earth
beneath the concrete

Reached up and softened   became fluid
and gentle   overcame the solidity
of rock   the structure of steel

Colored the landscape
concentric lines gave in to enjoy
the grace of the morning day

Became a solace as the
earth embraced them
and enfolded them in love

POEMS OUT OF
PHILOSOPHY

Madera

There is a time that catches you along the roadway,
at night when the sun is gone, where moon and stars

are even beyond your reach. You ride on the wide flat
but curved surface, treeline black against black hills.

You are in the reckoning where you reside with all others,
where each one sits solitary, distinct against the landscape

if there were one to see. It comes at odd times when
unexpected, when you are lost or wish to be, when you

wish to know and it is beyond your grasp. There it is the long
flat road curving, some of solid space, some of the ephemeral.

A Poem

Poems exist out there to be written but in these
times it may be for someone else to write of the pain,
the tragedy. There is much there but it may be for others

more closely involved to write of it, to reveal it to themselves
and to others. For me I am raw feeling that comes in
and goes out quickly, nothing stays long at the core.

It is a void, empty and full, moment-to-moment,
without time. In moments like these it is critical that some
hold in their mind, in their heart, in their daily living

the peace that has been called for over the centuries.
Some must do it no matter the "drums of war," no matter
the emotional chaos of grief, no matter the violence

that is perpetuated. If it is not held by some then there
is the chance it can disappear from our midst altogether.
Call on it, propagate it, live it, extend it into the world

and never let it disappear. Without it there is life but
there is no joy, no reason, purpose, no moments of bliss
that reveal us to ourselves, and to each other.

Flying to Chicago

We are rapidly fleeing the sun, charging into the dark night.
Decision and purpose demand that we leave the light behind.

We watch the outline of the setting sun retreat from definition,
into diffusion, distinctive etched lines in the red rock far below.

The cut away canyons and serrated edges of river rock walls,
fleeing the light, shortening the day. This is what we do when

flying into darkness, light becomes less, time shortens,
many colors dance just before dark. Lines of moisture

humped up in grey and white, pinks and purples, red upon red.
Every manner of blue escapes into the wall of dark. Great soft

continents, some rising, some falling, what manner of creature
inhabits this moist land. The gathering darkness, compression

of time, landscape of darkening dream.

Somewhere down there

Somewhere down there, through the moisture, the luminous haze
there is a single light, within the sphere of that light are others

like myself that I will never know. Their life, like mine will blaze
from this to that, something of us may mingle in the moisture

that even now lies between us. From the earliest time I have looked
for a single place where no footprint has been, like in the middle

of all those red rocks. Back in the dark I have looked into windows
and cars, seen people I will not know. My life will not know

the same ache that even now pierces their heart.

November 29th

Upon the Death of George Harrison

First, we were born the same year only weeks apart,
the heavens opened terribly at that moment.

We streamed through the opening when the world
was full of grief, and we share with others that grief.

'My sweet lord' he sang out and I like many others
found a momentary blissful connection.

Enlightenment some say is but a stringing together
of momentary blissful connections.

They come, they go and they alter us, only so
that we can realize who we are.

We string them together, he in his moment of birth
and in his moment of passing and all the songs in between.

Winter

It is deep in winter, I can tell, there is a hardness in my
chest, a sadness curves like a dark and lonely beast.
It may be time to stay with this sadness for a time.

There is a truth in the tangle that one must be with. It is
held in place by something unknown that will remain
unknown, only the shadow will be present. It will reveal

enough so that a truth will emerge, something needed but
just enough, something present but not the thing itself,
only glimpses that have enough, but only enough.

2001
Chico

I sit here in the Holiday Inn with the *Impressionists*
on PBS, this open notebook sitting and waiting, waiting ...

But nothing comes, fearful that if something is written
it will be many years before it is ready.

20, 30 years or longer its takes for what starts to be complete,
but 30 years is to long, and much needs to be done now.

And the cleft into the deep soil is not there, now
there is superficiality, business, professionalism,

homemaking. Too much gets in the way unless one is relentless
and lets nothing in the way, and that nothing includes the

world that is the subject of the work one wishes to do. Let
nothing in the way, keep absolutely clear about one's intent

and so, find from start to finish, that it is inevitable what
will happen and in the end nothing will emerge at all.

Clear deep place

Where has the clear deep place gone,
the one that was running with some emptiness.

To much is out there and what is in here
is no longer substantial enough to hold.

Has it been this way before when an era switches
from one to another like when there were dragons

and now there are none; like when there were
goddesses ordained and now they are not.

We must look elsewhere and then
give only hints and sighs.

March 18th

On the tarmac at Denver Airport waiting to de-ice –
heading for New Orleans and then Mississippi.
Yesterday our gathering in the hills. The communion

we made and the commitment to come. Laurene is beautiful.
I cannot take my eyes off of her beauty again. There is a
language that resides high up like the sun on the clouds

at 30,000 feet. Red and violet and magnificent, the language
we use brings new worlds into being, all of us gods
and goddesses. We know how to do this because it is our

nature to know. No one taught us, no one can take it away.
We know because that is what we are. We are those who
bring worlds into being with language. There never is a stumble,

each world is our creation, each thing our language of dreams,
each beauty the beauty that resides in our speaking and hearing.
What we call – the golden peak capped with gems, a love that

adorns us. We never forget, we wander the playground of the
world casting gems out in our speaking and there grows all the
beauty that we are, growing full bellied sculptures of love,

flying gold images of love, we speak and it is as it will be.

Young Lady at Denver Airport

It is the perfection of your roundness.

The placement of hips, the walk
that was inside you and came out.

The atmosphere like handfuls of pale
sun lit water. The warmth in your breasts
that shown like turbulence as you moved.

You revel in your life, you change your
surroundings to match your swelling,
your brightness to conceive. It was your

roundness, the roundness of attraction, the
roundness of hips, the roundness that encircles
your walk and your acceptance of revelation.

Meridian Mississippi

That name has some significance,
for now it sits outside my awareness.
Instead the landscape is rolling hills wooded
with Southern pine all of uniform size.

There is a sameness of landscape but
that is all that is the same. The locals
are friendly, too friendly, white and black,
a kind of open sweetness.

In the lobby an elderly volunteer lady
asks to help, I say, I am here temporary
from California. She helps me with my
need and then volunteers that people

should not be so negative towards
Mississippi. It is a beautiful place with
good people and people should not
be so negative towards this place.

Best Western

Sitting in this Best Western Motel room by the highway
in Meridian Mississippi, feeling both large and small
next to the largeness of the moment.

So odd to sit here watching the Oscars on TV, the bestowing
of the lifetime achievement award to Sidney Poitier, feeling
the enormity of it, strangely it is one of the great moments.

Sitting here in the emotional life of a great being chosen
by the great mystery to change everything. The life of feeling
makes sure we know it is about being human.

And he has a very large, rich, and very perfect emotional life
and I have the pleasure to well up into it with these people
in the still run down shacks of Meridian, who have yet to find

their own   perfect   way.

Unity

There is the pure experience of unity, of god, of the great
spirit, of the oneness of life in the diversity of existence.

Some few in history grasp it in perfection and convey it
but, alas, to most there are only snippets that come through

a solitary discipline, a religion, a culture, a tradition and we think
it is because of that discipline, religion, culture or tradition.

We think we have found the one and only route to that greatest
of all realizations, that perfect understanding, that life giving

experience. And then the downfall occurs – really, at that
moment when grace has passed, when the gift of bliss has

faded, only the route remains and then the frantic struggle to
retrieve it begins and the long and brutal history emerges

to create the conditions for that revelation to occur again.
But now the misunderstanding and the wrongful interpretations

and the great cycle of ignorance is upon us. We know of grace,
we know of bliss, we must, it seems, be in innocence and just

be thankful, stay in preparation, and wait.

Dark

Can we live only under a spreading cover of light.

Do we need just enough light to activate some little
known place in the brain, to know our place within

the spreading universe. Still, there are enough times
when the campfire goes out, laying alone under a

blue-black sky, surrounded by the black-green presence
of a great fallen sugar pine I knew in another life,

when pure, unfettered dark is enough, even a place
of glory, a completion of the roundness of existence.

Once in awhile we need a spreading cover of light
and a darkness that we can never truly reckon.

Lobelle
Meridian

So many names slip from my memory. My gift has been to
forget particulars and hence I have often lost that most precious.
But Lobelle has stayed, so quiet, so inward looking to a place

I have surely never seen and where I have surely never been.
But I have disciplined myself for so long to be with those
from a place other than mine, without harm, that in a rare

moment, now and then, they and I may greet. In her look
of fierce otherness, physically different beauty, so different
from what I know, in her days of despondence, she left a

hairline opening and we plunged through – the blues and reds
brightened like our own perfection. The light that comes off
a dark, dark background so full with what never gets spoken.

You let me see with the eye of the beloved and I am submerged
in your grace and I am thankful. Our meeting, a moment on
the so long path of all of us, now we continue on in love.

Falling in love

I know how wonderfully easy it is for me to fall in love.
It is beauty that does it. I don't fall in love with beauty
but beauty is the entrance to love. Mostly it is when
a woman has stood in her beauty, on purpose or not.

There was a morning when Kate was in this glowing
luminous place of beauty, she said in innocence,
"I won't be here long" and we both knew. She was
there both innocent and purposeful.

Some stand unknowing in beauty and I am graced with
knowing, like the young women in the Greeting Card
section at Barnes and Noble in Montgomery, simple and
elegant in a grey floor length dress cut up high in the back,

visible on a Sunday morning. Standing in her beauty,
purposeful but innocent of her effect. One hip drawn up,
the light from the large window illuminating from the outside.
I am in love, not so with her, and we will not meet,

but with her purpose, her willingness to bring beauty
into the world, to be the carrier of the goddess, purposeful
and innocent. And I have found beauty again so that
I may enhance the world in love.

An Understanding

Intention precedes understanding, whether of hours, days, years,
a life. Intention seeks an opening where the sedge grows, where
lodgepole may find roots, where breezes off the meadow may find
clear spaces to travel, where granite may offer its speckled

color and the cool mountain stream may invite feet to enter.
The journey begins and a roadbed somewhere rises in elevation.
Following undulations in foothills, traversing regions where the

mundane is seared with magic, where the day-to-day falls away.
Rising high the journey has given way, intention has receded
and deep and primordial breathing can occur, where breath
takes in air and the scent of pine, the language of earth,

the communication of beings human and not human.
There are gates one enters, intention, magic, breath, and a release
where granite mountains well up. One must breathe deep to catch

the beauty of old things hiding in diminished air. Breathe deep,
awakening our beauty self and we wake to ourselves these
surroundings. This place primitive, clear and known. It is a
pilgrimage and in between we forget and remember, celebrate

our first intention, approach exhaustion, release everything right
to the edge of the primordial mass, reabsorb wild mountains,
fill up with earth at high elevations. This place sits outside

our view, outside of consciousness, even outside of any life that
we could ever grasp, but it fills us fundamental, even foundational,
predicating everything on the chance to live, at all.

50 years with Allen and Jack

I can go back 50 years, I am one year old when Allen and Jack
meet   One year old when the bomb was dropped and the
atmosphere newly charged with realization and the molecular

dismantling of small children   circling the earth
dropping Zen particles on the heads of Allen and Jack
radiantly kissing their DNA informing the darkly streets at dawn

Zen voices thrown up into the morning cloud of raining light
carrying these children everywhere   when Allen and Jack
were poised to speak out against the apocalyptic dismantling
of children's radiant lives

raining on the streets of San Francisco and New York

I was one year old when prevailing winds carried my way

bless the children in their radiant death

surely it takes some time to come back
                          through a multitude of voices

Roots

We have roots deep into this earth where we reside
now if not always. We are beings of the middle world

where we reach out to others, some like ourselves,
some not. Strangers find us at times, some become

lovers and stay, some move on. We are beings
that reach for the simmering blaze of stars in the

Toulumne night sky. We may travel to that region, we shall see.
We have many friends who guide us and teach us on our

multiple journeys, some are beings from other than our own.
We listen to them as well on this not so comfortable journey.

AFTERWARD

War - Spring 2003

Highway 99 lays long and straight out towards the north
and the dark grey sky hung like an assemblage of goddesses.

Off to the eastern foothills the blue form mountains rise from black
primordial seams in the old earth into this and the next morning.

At this distance snow in the high country lays as if delivered
by ephemeral hands on the distant peaks and the new morning.

The flat bottom of spring clouds, still flooded with moisture,
maintains a poised countenance – rain could fall or not.

Once, on a 737, flying into New Orleans, I'm sure I saw sleeping spirits
in the weeping clouds outside my window – heads nodding this way

and that. I look toward the blue mountains at full but silent clouds
stretched across this so wide fertile valley held up against the peaks by

gentle hands. At the roadside long lines of dark green eucalyptus mark
off wide fields, deep emerald green, still soaked and cold from the

winter water. Far from the highway the blue mountains move with me
as the road unravels, fence rails and tree lines fall away with the

pounding rhythm of the black top. In the early morning a brilliant
orange sun rises from the eastern dessert behind the blue mountains

lays light to the coastal range. Farmland, vineyards, hedgerows glow
like new children, morning light illuminates this place as it has the high

dessert on the other side of the mountains. As it will the millennial blue
ocean to the west, as it has each part of the planet in the dark hours

before, as it will the rest of the planet to come. This day extends around
the earth, first this place and then another and another until it covers us

all and the spirits sleeping in the wet grey clouds everywhere.

106

New Orleans

Driving 28 miles across Lake Ponchartrain heading into
New Orleans. I look out my rear view mirror and see
two dark clouds dropping out of a grey sky, filled with rain,
all the way from Mississippi.

Listening to a local radio station as I enter the city and the
commentator says, "two tornados touch down on the north
shore of Lake Ponchartrain." I had been chased and I had
out run the beast but only by a few miles and a few minutes.

Driving the freeways around New Orleans I am struck by
the many signs indicating Hurricane Evacuation Routes,
all heading away from the water that surrounds the city.
I pull into the French Quarter, first time in 40 years,

and look for familiar landmarks; Bourbon Street and the
room my brother and I shared for two weeks at $14.00 a week.
Jackson Square and Col. Dwyer, the artist in his white suit
and fine goatee, gone no doubt but not forgotten by two

young artists. And Cafe du Monde. I had heard that it was
still there serving coffee and beignets only now under a
large awning, still the same, the same waiter in his stern face
and free spirit gone somewhere.

I remember way back being told that the city was below sea level
and all that held the water back were the levies. Two days before
Katrina, Ruth said, "oh, the city is only 6 feet below sea level and
the pumps will get the water out." She was born in New Orleans,

family and friends there now. Theresa was to fly in on Wednesday.
Hunter was missing on Monday. He was found safe a few days
later. They are all safe these distant friends but the water claimed
the land and the chest, the water rises in us as well.

They are wrapped in robes, the land is dessert, the homes in destruction. The sky is the same, pains enters the solar plexus and drives deep into the land. The language we cannot understand, voices make sounds and we know what they mean.

Eyes manifest and we are entered. Grief is a private affair we all share alone and together. It pulls on the water in our chest and works its way to overflowing. We can hold it back but not always. Sometimes we are inundated.

The mother for her child here and there
                    and we do not see the difference.

BIOPOETICA

Rainstick

I

I am in transport
rain
inside a bamboo rainstick

I am a traveling
forest

Rainstick
movement of the hand
shape of rain sounds in space
they dance together
rainstick and hand

II

I am young and old
I have seen many cycles
you have seen less

My girl says "take this"
she finds me something to cherish

Long feminine curves
texture of the ground
charged burnt tip

I find you a shape of elegance
a voice from the world
that is green

You are
the antlers of god
the twist of time
the end of tales

the forgotten place
the tangle
out of which
new forms come
you are broken and whole
united with the tree

from which you came
and lost to it
forever

You are the refuse
the remains
that which is discarded
a child
reaches to save you
and send you
off again
real in the world
now of dreams

III

We commune
like it or not
dark patches of
blown light
circus of thought
pass between us

A background
that has decayed
small quick movements

We sit or stand
walk or talk
and stories fall from us
like black sand
on the seaside cliffs

A relentless rhythm

We are a shape
or the visible
carriers of tales
we did not know
we would become

IV

There are points of pain
that keep me centered
in my body
I do not wish to experience

Is it you or me
the boundaries
that come and go
like morning from winter

Over and over I am not
that exquisite body in love
but this slightly
twisted shape that can't
quite tell whether
we are all together
moving through the net
of our lives

or me
alone
collapsing into
that irrevocable
inky black space
behind my eyes

Down the black stairs
hit like a hot blast
a green smell
old like the ending of seasons

Still vital
mixed
with the city that puts
its mark on the world

V

I sit
in meditation
wondering what will come

the sound of
a bus through the open window
the palm tree

It is hard to write on demand
usually a poem comes
in silence
in the dark
when the daytime
is shut down
and whole cities of people
wander semi-aware
in dream spaces

Today this city is underwater
we travel like mosquitoes in amber

Permission to have time
move as if it hadn't
been invented

Underwater cities
built in slow movement

VI

The colors don't come
when I put pastel to paper
what I see in my eye
can better be placed
when I use pencil to dark
magenta paper of mind

Vibration of purple running through

It is a singular part
of a journey of vibration

Just a step where the image can
bring itself into existence
something phenomenal
in the world of phenomena
whether primal colors
or a gray pencil to the
nondescript mind

VII

Centering a place where
vibrations arise
soul in concentric circles
radiant

Ring of skull

Ring of vibration

Ring of night and day

We are the ring
circling

Deep
in our center
the ring
brings two
into one place

VIII

Finding a place soundless
within sound
sound that lifts meaning

Rainstick
drum
flute
and the mountains of Nicaragua

landing in Managua
were the sun turns
many cycles

Where the light is set up
a heaping of tones
long laminating movement
a continuous stream
that is plucked
from the center of
a bell rung

Leaves in Eucalyptus
branches that reside in here
between ears
and the long world
unwinding

I am the branch of a tree
and the vibration rung

We never cease in the ringing
of moon and light
reflecting on water

All of this is what we are
the sound of a million
hands turning the rainstick
and the turning of leaves

IX

I sense movement
on and off the page

A rhythm takes us
where vibrations meet
and form the sound
that is our rhythm core

A dense place
of interlinking
vibrational patterns

A matrix
that with just the right push
we will move through
in ones and twos
'til the rainstick is silent
and all resistance is back there
ungraspable
circling and circling

X

I sense it like a beast empty of fire
no more urge to spill out fiercely

A lot of believing went into filling
that coiling at the base of my spine
it lies loosely

The journey needs to be unencumbered,
without laws, a goal, a direction,
so that the outcome will be the journey itself
nothing to prejudice the recall

Feet disappearing into Paleolithic mud
beating earth shaking its axis
righting itself

The tool of mind the mass encumbrance—
in its place a whirling band of gluey substance
interweaving at least this planet but likely others
certainly the moist interior

    XI

Justice insures each element
the chance to reach completion
again and again

Rock is rock
foundation for cathedral
rock cannot be rock

Justice returns foundation
over eons to sand, seabed and rock
to be rock fulfillment
rock people and the wisdom of rock

The short and the long
we live both sunrise to sunrise
eon to eon

Justice holds each time in place

Justice dislodged must come back
in time
because that is what holds time in place
time is held up
when justice is lost

We stagger in the journey
encumbered
until justice is righted again of itself

    XII

The last time I talked to her
over the phone
she said laughing
what crazy thing are you doing now

I told her and said
I can do nothing else

Her children are as old as mine

My space is less contained
it spreads out, fascination gone
nothing fastened to walls
to hold them up frighteningly

My early pursuit of art music religion
came from before death

Staring out a solitary mind struck off
returning to the common frequency

Intervening
straining watching travelers

A large group gathered on a wide lawn
painting tennis shoes, selling buttons
the whole crowd calling out
the same spatial arrangement of wholes
calling to be filled
like a blanket woven of eternal light

The walls lurched
the beast turned side to side

XIII

The children came early
unfinished in electronic gadgets
all naturalness gone
except two Indian doctors
who oversaw electron people
complete the work

Finally released from wires
they return to completion

XIV

She and I split a few years later
unable to take on an alien form
the directive couldn't be altered
the pain reached a great wall

Everything went as it should
the plateau was very small
once the whole was full

A drumbeat fell from her feet
and she said no

We flew like grasshoppers in a windstorm
the endings have been constant

They continue with walls falling
that were not ready to fall
Old walls coming back
that were turning into ancestors

It was fatal
the glory carved in the night

The trail got cold
the leaves lay thick and labor a detour

A single error at exactly the time
a question that lead to a compromise

All the exactness streamed in and
the coil sprang to life twitching

     XV

There are three arcing pulls
always three
it is the number
of the highest completion

Because it is an odd number
it accounts for the great diversity

All things subsumed

The loved and beloved
and the offspring,
the many that fill the sea

Humpback whale on another journey
small fish in schools barracuda alone
starfish crab and lobster sailing the bottom
plankton and squid gathered by the millions
tuna and dolphin diving together in danger

The many that fill the sky

Trees with roots into oxygen

Vulture climbs to thinner
and thinner regions
exhilarating daring high

Small lungs pump blood
lesser air
charged excitement
streaming vision
blues and yellows, violet and red
nerves transmit
end feather moved by
unheard molecules

The many that fill the wild land

Holes burrowed into sandy creek bank
fox drawing back covered by earth
released into memory
filling up caves of old thought

Deer meeting on high mountain meadow
whole language transmitted on scent and smell

The understanding of another journey
through Sage and Buck Brush Bull Pine
White Fir Torrey Pine and Lodgepole

The journey a circle of hunger
that is there time and time after

Risen from everything is the loved and beloved
the two contained in everything
the resolving out
the poles that give rise
the hunger inside the circle
the dynamic that must be resolved
and must give

The two that become one
the loved and beloved
that resolve into love
when they are forgotten

The singularity
the one that is all one
the one that is the circle of love
that is the container
that is contained

It is three that are two that is one

The breast opens and the beast
empties out

The emergence is all that is left
it sails forward and we disappear

XVI

At Dungeoness Point
we held on and this time
in the warm grey evening
she disappeared in me

I had the presence of mind to note it
but not the gratitude
to thank her

XVII

Either we are without dignity
or we are held to the present
ready for the next movement
exactly ready
the moment when the call is out
or dignity has been lost

I have let go
it is time
I will love or not
I will work or not

I will be empty
or not
but I wait

The journey has no end
but at this time justice has been covered
and everything is far out of time

I lay in your bed
new paint on the walls
the floor also new
and primal

I had the will to change the destiny of rocks
and now they are in tears

The bed is warm and candles
sanctified in the temple invade the walls

You carry the hills where temples originate

I have let go this time
and the rock people are waiting

I have given up

Let's you and I give in
you are my beloved
your greenery surrounds me in the daylight

and your emerald stones
bury me in the night

124

We have once again cast the many out
into the sea the sky   and the wild land
where they will travel
with feet ground in tiny stones of light

Now I wish only to lie in your bed
where your sacred earth
your body straddles me

We huddle as justice
realigns the world people

XVIII

You bath me
and drain my pain
into an endless reservoir
of light

Hot breath
filling me
magic body
sacred sister

In the purple morning I
drop into a far place

You the body of habitation
nectar of silk mouth
enfolding new form of the void

Body of radiance

Atomic breasts
curving wild energy
of lust and love

We in darkness
black night
the hidden room
love not discovered
the undoing
the moment before

The sage seeks and cannot find

You invite me to the comfort
of your belly
sucked deep in your purpose

We lie together and find
the nothing of lust
window of emptiness
purpose of yellow and violet
love of the
covered women
the end of the real

Man empty
and alive

Push back the flow of history

We are magic that stops all
but the flow of void

We are the sex of love

The sex of bodies gone radiant
but gone

        Gone   Gone

Bio

i have tried over the years to find a bio that fits and is suitable and
i have failed   still i was oddly blessed with a name that opens vast
landscapes so this name is my bio

john is found in more than 85 variants from many countries of the
world juan jean jianni ivan jan johan jon jahn jack johnny
joao juanita juanito joan ivanovich jonathon johannes
joannes johnson jock ovan yohanan ioannes jeannot jehan

john is found in peculiar reference in the most unlikely settings
as reference for toilet - going to the john   as the prostitute's liaison
- the hooker's john   biblically as - john the beloved   john means
yahwah   there have been 114 saints named john and an infinite
number of the hooker's johns

john the baptist   don juan   ivan the terrible   joan of arc   john muir
jack of hearts   jack of all trades (master of none)   jean valjean
johnny apple seed   john doe   johan sabastian bach   iron john
john henry   john of the cross   johnny cake   john's wort

in a room full of people   john is called out and many respond   it is
said that names are vibrations of the person   in some cultures one
waits to hear the essence of a person before a name is given

i have worked and lived in the city   hills and mountains including
yosemite throughout my life i have published *dark hills and wild
mountains* and with tomás gayton *two races one face two faces
one race* chapbooks *this warrior is always at peace* and *uzumite*

my bio is really in the work itself   along with the circumstance of the
poems i have raised a family of four children   Neyah Miles Devon
and Kiirsti   live gratefully on a piece of property with Laurene
and on ocassion publish poetry books by poets who
have something to say and the artistry to say it

the danger in living for a time is that one can accept that life is merely
a mix of the good and the ill   though this seems true yet we must
as Ted Kardash Taoist Priest once said in a discussion of Taoist
Philosophy   recognize that the Tao is good and follow that path

Books from Poetic Matrix Press

TRIAL & ERROR
prose poems by Arthur W. Campbell
ISBN 978-09789597-4-6 $16.00

News of the Day
Poems of the Times by John
ISBN 978-09789597-3-9 $16.00

The Unequivocality of a Rose
a poem by Joel Netsky
ISBN 978-09789597-1-5 $15.00

In A Dress Made Of Butterflies
poems by Sandra Lee Stillwell
ISBN 978-0-9789597-0-8 $15.00

Of One and Many Worlds
Buddhist poems by Rayn Roberts
ISBN 0-9714003-9-3 $15.00

Nature Journal with John Muir
edited by Bonnie Johanna Gisel
ISBN 0-9714003-7-7, hardcover $20.00
ISBN 0-9714003-5-0, paperback $16.00

The Lost Pilgrimage Poems
A book of poetry by Joseph D. Milosch
ISBN 0-9714003-8-5 $15.00

Winds of Change/
Vientos de Cambio
bilingual poems Tomás Gayton
ISBN: 0-9714003-6-9 $15.00

Change (will do you good)
by poet Gail Rudd Entrekin
ISBN 0-9714003-4-2 $15.00

Merge with the river
by Yosemite poet James Downs
ISBN 0-9714003-2-6 $14.00

Driven into the Shade
by Brandon Cesmat
2003 San Diego Book Award Poetry
ISBN 0-9714003-3-4 $14.00

dark hills and wild mountains
poems by john
ISBN 0-9714003-0-X $14.00

Solstice
by Kathryn Kruger
ISBN 0-9714003-1-8 $7.00

www.ingramcontent.com/pod-product-compliance
Lightning Source LLC
Chambersburg PA
CBHW071945100426
42736CB00042B/1990

9 780978 959739